MY HOUSE
MEMORIES OF THE CHICAGO HOUSE MUSIC CULTURE

Entertainer Dave Risqué

BY DEREK "SMOKIN" JONES

Flying Turtle Business Publications
an imprint of
Flying Turtle Publishing
Hammond, Indiana

This book is the author's homage to and memory of a specific music genre and the culture it spawned. Uncredited pictures are from the author's personal collection of photographs and memorabilia. All other photographs are used by permission. Please see the last page additional permissions information.

Product photos are trademarked and are endorsed by the author, without compensation.

The publisher does not have any control over third-party websites or their content.

Manufactured in the United States of America

ISBN-13: 978-0-9911378-79

Introducing Derek "Smokin" Jones

A little about me:

I'm a native Chicagoan, born on the southside. I fell in love with House Music in 1980. Like most original Chicago House Music lovers, I listened to WBMX FM 102.7 on the dial. WBMX had a legendary DJ team called the Hot Mix Five that played mainstream House Music and imports.

House Music in Chicago was primarily underground and got its roots from Disco. But I love all forms of the music. Just listening to House Music made me at peace with the world. It touched my soul and ministered to me in so many ways.

House Music has given me a long career, with more than 30 years as a Touring DJ, Producer and Record Label Owner. I put my first record out in 1985 on Rodney Bakerr's label Rockin House Records. The song was *"Homeboy."* From there, I produced for legendary Chicago Trax Records owned by Larry Sherman.

This is my memory book and a salute to all DJs, producers, artists, and fans—past and present— keeping the House Music culture alive. In this book

DJ Derek "Smokin" Jones

you will see some of our history displayed in photos and captions. I wish I could get everything and everyone in this book but that would be way too much for one book. This is a just a glimpse of what made Chicago the greatest home of House Music.

I did this in a scrapbook style and I hope you enjoy it.
I hope it will bring back some joyful memories to
Chicago House Music lovers around the word.

Derek "Smokin" Jones live at Knockouts

Derek "Smokin" Jones performing on the Global Music DJs show

**Derek "Smokin" Jones
first single**

First Album

One of my popular logos

Second 2015 Album Collaboration

Record Label logo

Bad Boy Bill of the Hot Mix 5 & Derek "Smokin" Jones

Old School House Head theme

DJ Darryl Fortyplus Hopkins,
fan Charlene Williams & Derek
"Smokin" Jones

DJ International TV interview

Logo

R&B song "Movin On," produced by Derek Smokin Jones & BJ featuring: J Mitchell

What is House Music?

House music is a genre of electronic dance music that originated in Chicago in the 1980s House Music quickly spread to other cities and countries, each creating its own scenes. Because of its popularity, multiple genres and styles of House Music were created, such as Deep House, Soulful, Underground, Acid, Dance, Gospel House, Tech House, Tribal and many more.

The Godfather Of House Music

Frankie Knuckles

January 18, 1955 Bronx, New York City – March 31, 2014 Chicago IL

Residences: His best known Chicago clubs residencies were The Warehouse and The Playground

Frankie and his Grammy

U.S. President Barack Obama & Frankie

Chicago street sign honoring Frankie

**You will be missed by all of us.
May your memory and your music live on.**

The Legendary Ron Hardy

May 8, 1958 – March 2, 1992

Best known DJ residencies in Chicago: The Muzic Box and Sauers

Ron & Robert Williams

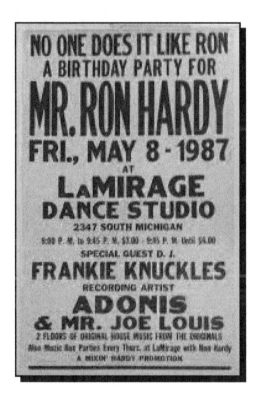

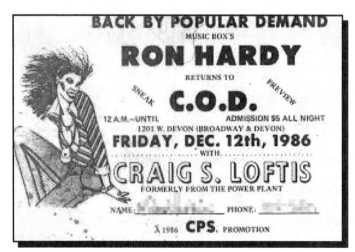

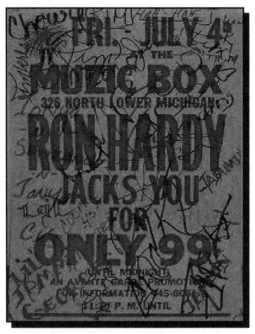

You will forever be the King of Chicago Disco.
Thank you for being a great friend and mentor.

THE HOT MIX FIVE

The Hot Mix 5 Chicago IL, American DJ team Chosen by WBMX program director Lee Michaels in 1981. The founding members of the Hot Mix 5 were Farley "Funkin" Keith (later became Farley Jackmaster Funk), Mickey "Mixin" Oliver, Ralphie Rosario, Kenny "Jammin" Jason, Scott "Smokin" Silz.

Chicago Honorary Street Signs

Scott Silz, Ralphi Rosario, Farley Keith

THE KING OF HOUSE

January 25, 1962 – Present
Credits: Producer, Touring DJ, Chicago Trax Records artist
Genre: House Music & Gospel House Music
Nominations: Brit Award for British Video
Original Member of the Hot Mix 5 DJ team
Best known Tracks: Love Can't Turn Around, House Nation, Funking with the Drums.

Thank you for teaching me how to DJ.

**Farley took the time one evening in 1983
to come to my home
to teach me and one of my childhood friends,
Jeff Green, how to DJ.
It was the greatest night of my life and
will forever be one of my best memories.**

Chicago Trax Records

Chicago Trax Records was the second label I produced for. Founded in 1983 by Larry Sherman and Screamin Rachael Cain. This label was one of the driving forces for house music in Chicago and around the world.

Just a few artist credits:

Marshall Jefferson: The House Music Anthem "Move Your Body"

Derek "Smokin" Jones : "Take Me"

Adonis: "No Way Back"

Eric Bell: "Your Love"

Larry Heard (Mr. Fingers): "Can You Feel It"

Frankie Knuckles: "Baby Wants to Ride"

Larry Sherman CEO

Rachael Cain Co-owner and Current CEO

Frankie & Rachael

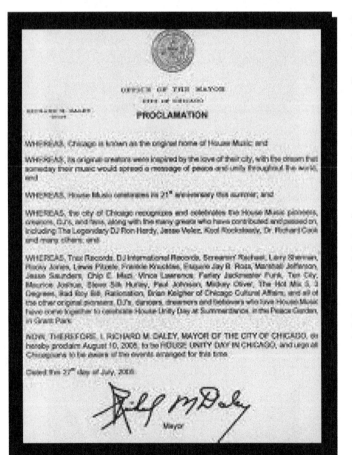

City of Chicago House Unity Day Proclamation.

The document declared August 10th as House Unity Day in Chicago. The declaration was done Aug 10, 2005. It coincided with the 21st birthday of Chicago Trax Records.

The event was organized by Brian Keigher, program director of Chicago's Department of Cultural Affairs.

Also, big thanks to Rachael Cain for her hard work.

This is one of the most popular Trax record covers, showing the Chicago skyline.

DJ International

DJ International Records was founded in 1985 by musician Rocky Jones.

Some artists and producers that helped put DJ on the map:

Steve "Silk" Hurley, Chip E, Fingers INC, Tyree Cooper, Bam Bam, Fast Eddie, Sterling Void, Kenny "Jammin" Jason, Frankie Knuckles, Joe Smooth, Adonis, Danny "Sweet D" Wilson & Richard Patterson aka (Full House)and Farley "Jackmaster" Funk

Rocky Jones founder and CEO

DJ International Records logo

Rocky Jones Hard at work filming DJ TV.

**A young Rocky Jones & Farley "Funkin" Keith,
aka (Farley "Jackmaster" Funk)**

TEN CITY album cover

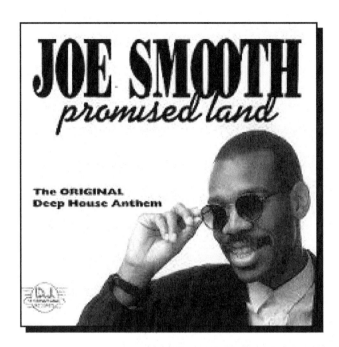

ROCKIN' HOUSE RECORDS

Founder and CEO Rodney Bakerr

Rockin' House Logo

Rodney holding the classic Roland electronic drum machine. This was one type of drum used by Chicago House Music producers, and one of the most popular drums used in the 80s and 90s for House Music production

A young Mike Dunn & Rodney

Chicago House Style

House is a feeling and part of that was how we dressed. Our typical dress code was very simple. Popular blue jeans, t-shirt, gym shoes or flats, and a sweat towel in our back pockets. But then came the 80s prep style of fashion. Coach, Izod, Polo, Swatch, Gucci, Levi Jeans, Giorgio Armani, (GA) Oxford shirts, K-Swiss. Well, you'll see and remember.

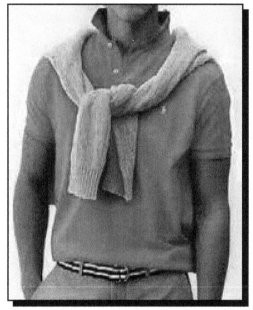

Preppy Polo™ style

K-Swiss™

Deck shoes

Coach™ Belt with tag

The famous Penny Loafers

Guess™ Pullover

The Swatch™ Watch

Coach™ Purse with tag

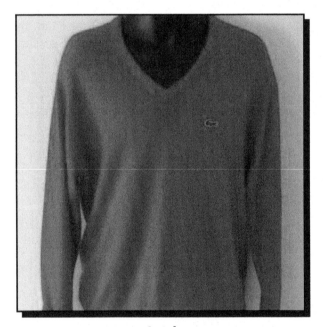

Izod

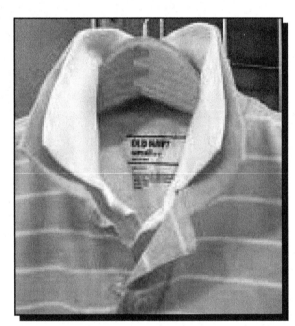

Double Polo Shirts

We had to smell good too!

Oh, can't forget the Duck shoes we called steppers.

Moccasins

SOME OF OUR FAVORITE SNACKS

Lunchroom cookies aka Butter Cookies

Pickles & Peppermint

Candy Necklace

Some Flyers & Places

The Warehouse night club

Some of the best House Music concerts and performances by DJs Ron Hardy and Frankie Knuckles where held at the historic Chicago Theatre

A Few More Memorable Flyers and Logos

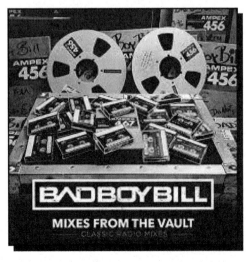

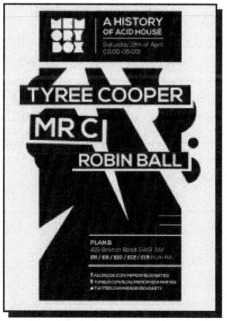

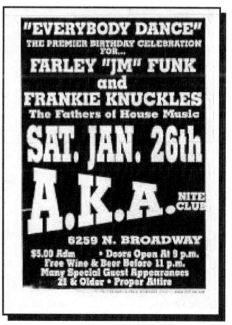

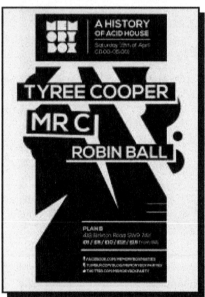

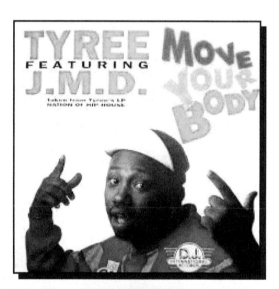

CLUB DRUGS

Drugs are NEVER good, but they were and still are part of club culture. I lost friends to some of these drugs.

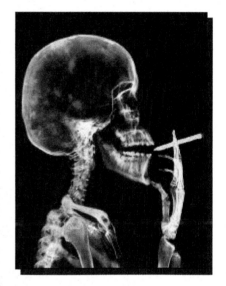

TOP OF THE PILL POPPERS

Number of statins or statin-like doses given daily per 1,000 people in 2011

	#	Country			#	Country	
	1	Australia	137		13	Czech Republic	92
	2	United Kingdom	130		13	France	92
	2	Slovakia	130			OECD average	91
	4	Belgium	122		15	Spain	90
	5	Norway	116		16	Portugal	88
	6	Denmark	115		17	Iceland	80
	7	Luxembourg	112		18	Sweden	77
	8	Canada	109		19	Italy	72
	9	Netherlands	101		20	Germany	68
	10	Hungary	98		21	South Korea	34
	11	Finland	95		22	Estonia	32
	12	Slovenia	93		23	Chile	10

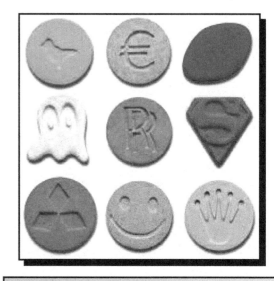

Club Drugs

- Primarily used by youth and young adults at dance or all night parties and bars
- Typically either stimulants or sedative-hypnotics
- None are benign – all can cause serious health problems or death
- Some are used in the commission of sexual assault

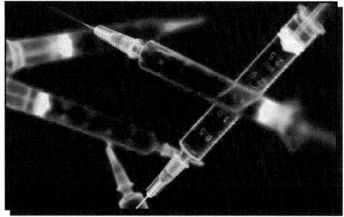

DJS' and PRODUCERS' TOOLS OF THE TRADE

Linn Drum Machine™

Roland Drum Machine™

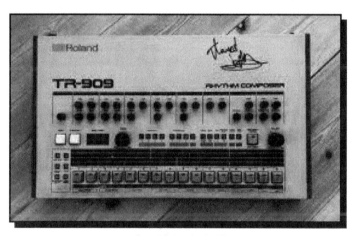

Roland TR-909™

Most of our tracks where on 4-track recorders

The Mirage Keyboard and the Roland DX7 where favorites among Track makers in the 80s

We did most of our recording and making of tracks in the 80s in our bedrooms and basements. Not shown: the 808 and the 606 drum machines. They were popular for Acid tracks.

MIXERS TURNTABLES AND CONTROLLERS PAST AND PRESENT

Technics™ Turntables curved and straight-arm are the most popular DJ turntables in the world

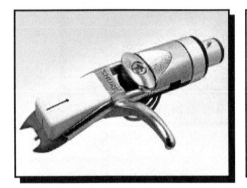  

Most popular among DJs where the Shure™ and Stanton™ needles used on turntables

This small device would hook to the head shell of a needle and collect the dust off a record to keep the needle clean and clear. It also kept the needle from sliding across the record from too much dust being collected under it

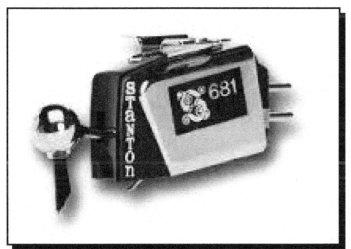

The Stanton™ Dust Cleaner above attached to this needle

OLD & NEW SCHOOL DJ MIXERS

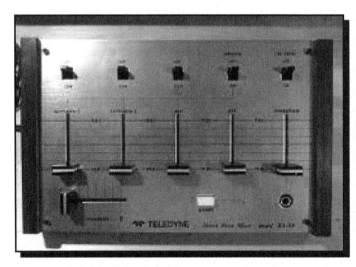
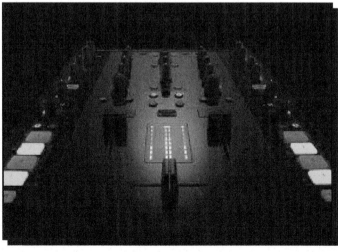

Above is a laptop view of DJ software called Serato™

DJs today use CDs, DJ controllers and USB memory sticks to carry their favorite music. With software such as Virtual DJ™, Serato™, and Native instruments™, DJ controllers are built to help DJs edit and sample music live. Much different from the past when DJs had to physically manipulate vinyl records on the turntables.

DJ Controllers

Today, all the records you see on these shelves can be stored on USB memory sticks and CDs

CDs

USB Memory sticks

Pioneer™ CDJ-2000 Player

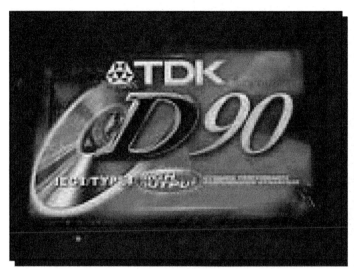
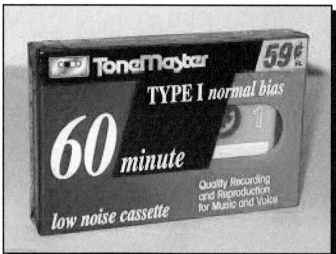

Cassette tapes, old school favorites for saving music

Let not forget the old Reel to Reel recorder and DAT machines (Digital Audio Tape)

24 track recorder Mastering tape machine

DJs pick different types of headphones for sound & comfort

CELEBRATING SOME OF CHICAGO'S DJS AND FANS

**DJ Wayne Williams of the Chosen Few DJs
Lymuel Ivester Jr. CEO of Old School House Head Brand
DJ Alan King of the Chosen Few DJs**

DJ Alicia & Sheila Djred Thurman

Recording artist J.R. Jordan

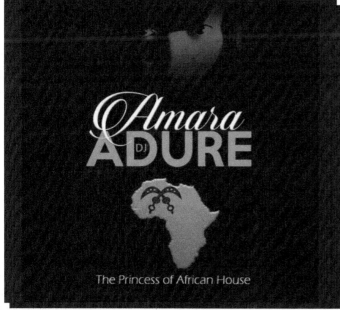

**House Music fans at the
Annual Chosen Few picnic**

Recording Artist Curtis McClain & friends

No Ratz DJs

DJs Derrick Carter, Martin Kouba and Bridget Marie

DJ Leonard Remix Roy & Producer Derrick Sales

DJ Dion Hunter

The original members of the first annual 2015 House Head Retreat in Galena, Illinois

Chosen Few DJs Alan King, Wayne Williams and Mike Dunn in Chicago's Daley Plaza

DJs Darryl Williams and Eric Bell,
Chicago VIP Picnic

DJ and Music Producer Titan Davis

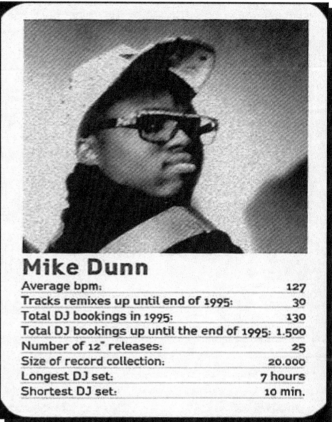

Mike Dunn

Average bpm:	127
Tracks remixes up until end of 1995:	30
Total DJ bookings in 1995:	130
Total DJ bookings up until the end of 1995:	1.500
Number of 12" releases:	25
Size of record collection:	20.000
Longest DJ set:	7 hours
Shortest DJ set:	10 min.

Loyal fan Angie Peña

Ain't nothing but a House Party

DJ/Producer AL HotMix Holmes

DJ/Producer Mike Deshawn Latiker

Robert Williams founder of
Chicago's Warehouse night club

DJ/ Producer Paul Johnson

DJ/Producer Gene Hunt

DJ/Producer Mike Dunn

DJ Kris Hutchinson

DJ Celeste Alexander

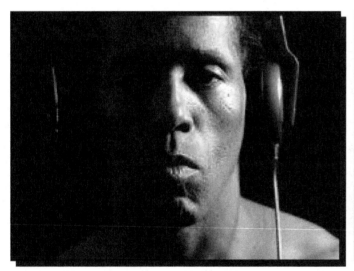

DJ/Producer Lil Louis

DJ/Producer Corky Traxman Strong

Grammy award winning DJ/Producer
Steve "Silk" Hurley

DJ Hula Mahone

Grammy Award Winning DJ/Producer Maurice Joshua

DJ/Producer Marshall Jefferson

DJ/Producer Jesse Saunders

DJ Rocky Floyd

Chicago recording artist Kym Sims

Chicago recording artist Karen Gordon aka Dajae

CHICAGO'S VERY OWN HOUSE MUSIC MagaZINE 5

5 Magazine logo

Founder/ DJ Czarina Mirani aka Czboogie

DJ Sundance

DJ "Lil" John Colman, Soul 106.3 FM Chicago

DJ Mike Dunn & DJ Lil John

HOUSE MUSIC QUOTES

NOT EVERYONE UNDERSTANDS HOUSE MUSIC

GOD IS A DJ
LIFE IS A
DANCEFLOOR
LOVE IS
THE RHYTHM
YOU ARE
THE MUSIC

I ♥ HOUSE MUSIC

MUSIC GIVES A SOUL TO THE UNIVERSE, WINGS TO THE MIND, FLIGHT TO THE IMAGINATION, AND LIFE TO EVERYTHING.

4 DA LOVE OF HOUSE MUSIC!
NO 1 WIL STOP ME 4RM
LISTNG 2 HOUSE MUSIC BCOZ I
WAZ BORN 4 DIS ND DIS IS MY
ONLY HOPE I HVE!   HOUSE
MUSIC MADE ME WHO I AM
2DAY! BY CRAZY DJ
MJOVISTO!

QuotePix.com

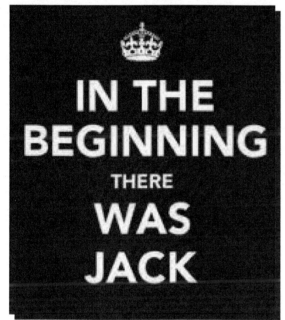

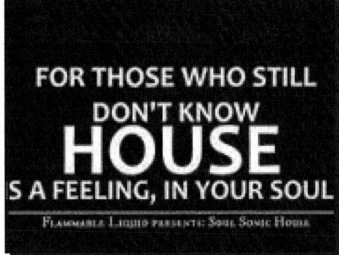

Thanks to all who create the slogans we love!
And thank you all for sharing this
House Music journey with me!

SPECIAL RECOGNITION

DJ Rick Johnson
DJ Steve Poindexter
DJ Hugo Hutchinson
DJ Rob Waite • WIIT 88.9 Fm
DJ James Big Daddy House
DJ Angie Stone
DJ Pharris Thomas • The Heavy
   Hitter, Power 92 FM Chicago
Bobby Q Bobby • WKKC Radio
   Chicago
DJ Lil John Coleman • 106.3 FM
   Chicago
DJ Nicky Divine
Steve Silk Hurley • JM Silk
Recording Artist Keith Nunnally •
   JM Silk
DJ Emanuel Pippin
DJ Jay Hill
DJ Craig Loftus
DJ Tony T
DJ Boo Williams
DJ Jammie 326

DJ Producer Glen Underground
DJ Mickey Calvin
DJ Kenny Ray
Recording Artist Sheree Hicks
Recording Artist Byron Stingily
DJ Rocky Floyd
DJ Fiddy Millz
Music Producer Mathew Yates
Recording Artist Kim Jay
DJ Vernell Byrd
DJ Rex Racer
Recording Artist Harry Dennis
Recording Artist Sterling Void
DJ Karen Lucas aka DJ Michele K
DJ/Producer Stacy Kidd
DJ/Producer Bruce Ivery
DJ Craig Debonair Davis
Craig Abron
Benji Espinoza • A&R/DJ
   International Records
George Daniels • George's Music
   Room

PROMOTIONS

Reginald Corner • The Way We Were
John Hunt • Gucci Promotions
Mario Durham • MDG Live
Park Avenue
Byron Taylor • LB Productions Inc
Ron Watkins • Da House Spot

PERMISSIONS

Photographs Used with Permission of*:

Rachael Cain • Chicago Trax™ Records

Gene Hunt, Steve Poindexter, Rodney Bakerr • Rockin House® Records

Scott Silz • Hot Mix Five©

Karen Gordon AKA Dajae, Curtis McClain, Eric Bell,
Marshall Jefferson, Czarina Mirani • 5 Magazine

Hector Escobedo • Pioneer Corporation

*Uncredited pictures are from the author's personal collection of
photographs and memorabilia.

CPSIA information can be obtained
at www.ICGtesting.com
Printed in the USA
LVOW06s1622270317
528631LV00036B/1379/P